Straight
from the
Heart

for COUPLES

Straight From the Heart
for Couples

by
Richard Exley

Tulsa, Oklahoma

Straight From the Heart for Couples
ISBN 1-56292-094-4
Copyright © 1995 by Richard Exley
P.O. Box 54744
Tulsa, Oklahoma 74155

Published by Honor Books
P.O. Box 55388
Tulsa, Oklahoma 74155

Presented to:

_____

On the Occasion of:

_____

Presented by:

_____

Date:

_____

DEDICATION

To Douglas and Leah Starr,
now and forever.

∽

Contents

1 A Gift and a Discipline 11

2 Bonding 17

3 The Music of Marriage 23

4 Celebrating the Ordinary 31

5 Love Letters 39

6 Love and Anger 47

7 Keeping Romance in Marriage 55

8 Love for a Lifetime 63

Epilogue 71

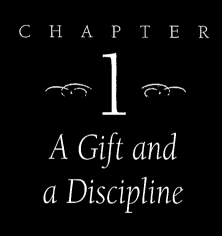

CHAPTER

1

*A Gift and
a Discipline*

"*In reality, marriage is the most demanding endeavor of our lives. It is both a gift and a discipline.*"

Chapter 1

A Gift and a Discipline

Marriage begins, for most of us, with bright expectations – and well it should.

Parents shed bittersweet tears of painful happiness. Friends laugh, hug our necks and congratulate us. It's a special moment, holy and happy.

We have vowed our faithfulness "till death do us part." We belong to each other as we have never belonged to anyone before. We relate to one another in a way no one else can ever relate to either of us, or we to them.

She is my only wife. I am her only husband.

In all of our other relationships, we are one among many. One child among several children in our family, one friend among many friends, one student among many students, one of many players on the team, one of several employees on the job, one of many...

Not now, not here! For the first time ever, I am the only one to her, and she is the only one to me.

In many ways, marriage is a miracle. It is not a miracle in the sense that it happens supernaturally without effort or investment on our part. Rather, it is a miracle in the sense that in spite of our immaturity and selfishness, in spite of our independence and differing personalities, we truly become one, at least for a time.

I do not mean to suggest that we will always be happy, or that we will never know moments of despair or even rage. In truth, there will be the inevitable conflicts, little hurts and not so little hurts, bitter quarrels and haunting fears. Pressures too, which pull at us, causing us to drift apart. Silences beneath our words, and loneliness, the kind of loneliness that only those who have known the blessed oneness can imagine. Holy moments too when forgiveness gives birth to intimacy, when the silences and the separation are put behind us, and once again we know who we are and where we belong.

In truth, marriage is a lot like life – full of contradictions and conflicts, but for all of that still so blessed, oh so blessed.

It has its moments – anniversaries and other special days, as well as unscheduled surprises and unexpected kindnesses, little gestures of love that set the heart to singing – but for the most part, it's more pedes-

trian. And it's those mundane details that mold the character of our relationship. Little things, which at first glance hardly seem worth mentioning. Yet as the years go by, they become daily rituals.

I mean, whoever speaks of the simple pleasure of coming home to familiar sounds — the hum of the vacuum cleaner, bath water running, conversation from the other room — yet these are the sounds of marriage. And the smells — skin cream and shampoo, clothes fresh from the dryer, furniture polish and coffee brewing. Ordinary things easily taken for granted, hardly noticed, until shared in marriage.

While preaching on the subject of marriage one Sunday morning, I told my congregation that my wife Brenda and I had a special song, "our" song as it were.

"Why," I said, "just thinking about it now, I can almost hear it."

I had cued the sound man ahead of time, and at that very moment he rolled the tape. You can imagine the startled looks I received from my congregation as the melodious voice of John Denver floated through the sanctuary. Then they settled in to eavesdrop on "our" song.

When the song was finished, I asked them to remember the lyrics, the things Denver had sung about. They were ordinary things, every one — supper on the stove, a storm across the valley, the sound of a truck out on the four-lane, the passing of time — hardly the stuff of love songs.

Yet, in another sense, in the truest sense, it was. For a marriage cannot be made only of special times. They are too few. By their very nature, they are rare. That's what makes them special. Marriage and family have to be made out of sturdier stock, common stuff, made somehow special by the love of those who share it.

In reality, marriage is the most demanding endeavor of our lives. It is both a gift and a discipline. God gives us each other, and the tools for cultivating our blessed oneness, but it is up to us to work the soil of our relationship all the days of our lives.

CHAPTER

2

Bonding

" 'Bonding... [is] the emotional covenant that links a man and woman together for life. It is the specialness which sets those two lovers apart from every other person on the face of the earth.. '"

Chapter 2

Bonding

Whether you are newlyweds or an "old married couple," you can undoubtedly recall your wedding day.

She remembers it in great detail — the music, the flowers, the ceremony. He remembers it as a kind of blur, important to be sure, but indistinct, except for the radiant smile of his bride as she came down the aisle on her father's arm.

Weeks and months of planning were over far too quickly, and the two of you fled beneath a deluge of rice and best wishes from family and friends. Returning from your honeymoon, you discovered that you were far better prepared for the wedding than for marriage.

Although the bride and her mother had spent months planning every detail of the wedding, they had hardly given a thought to the marriage itself. The groom, while not nearly as concerned with the details of the wedding, was equally guilty of assuming that marriage would somehow take care of itself.

In retrospect, it seems tragically nearsighted to invest so much time and energy in the wedding, which lasts only two or three hours, while giving the marriage, which is for a lifetime, hardly a second thought.

Still, what's done is done. Prepared or not, it is now time to address the work of marriage.

The first task facing newlyweds is the transfer of allegiance: "For this reason a man will leave his father and mother and be united to his wife, and they will become one flesh."[1]

This transfer of allegiance is necessary before a husband and wife can truly bond with one another.

"Bonding," according to Dr. Desmond Morris, "[is] the emotional covenant that links a man and woman together for life. It is the specialness which sets those two lovers apart from every other person on the face of the earth."[2]

This blessed oneness is embryonic to begin with. That is, it is true in the spirit of the relationship, but not in the reality of day-to-day life. Two separate and distinct individuals are not suddenly made one simply

---

[1] Genesis 2:24 (italics added).

[2] Desmond Morris, Intimate Behavior (New York: Random House, 1971), p. 73.

because a minister pronounces them husband and wife. They become one flesh. It takes time and commitment, not to mention love and hard work.

On the eve of her wedding, one young woman received a letter from her father in which he wrote:

"After tomorrow you will be Gary's wife. Our daughter still, but not in the same way, not ever again. From the moment the minister pronounces you husband and wife, your first allegiance, your first loyalty, will belong to Gary. Our home will no longer be your home. With Gary you will now make a new home of your own. You must leave us emotionally before you can cleave to your husband, before you can truly become one flesh with him."

This does not mean that the newlywed couple is no longer in relationship with their parents, only that the parent-child relationship has changed. Whereas, before, it was "the" primary relationship, it has now become a secondary one. Still important, to be sure, but not as important. Now the husband-wife relationship is preeminent.

The aforementioned father went on in his letter to address this issue as well. He wrote:

"Marriage is what you make it. Under God, it must be the most important relationship in all your life. If your marriage is good, you can overcome anything – financial adversity, illness, rejection, anything. If it is not good, there is not enough success in the world to fill the awful void. Remember, nothing, absolutely nothing, is more important than your marriage, so work at it with love and thoughtfulness all the days of your life.

"Guard it against all intruders. Remember your vows. You have promised, before God and your families, to forsake all others and cleave only to each other. Never allow friends, or family, or work or anything else to come between you and your beloved.

"Marriage is made of time, so schedule time together. Spend it wisely in deep sharing. Tell him your whole heart. Listen carefully and with understanding when he in turn shares his heart with you. Spend it wisely in fun – laugh and play together. Go places and do things together. Spend it wisely in worship – pray together. Spend it wisely in touching – hold each other – be affectionate.

"Remember, a song isn't a song until you sing it, a bell isn't a bell until you ring it and love isn't love until you give it away, so give all of your love to each other all the days of your life."

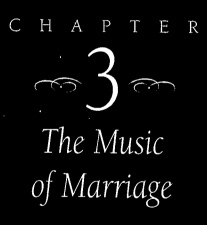

CHAPTER

3

*The Music
of Marriage*

*" ...communication is the
music of marriage."*

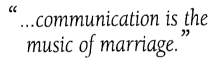

Chapter 3

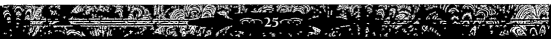

The Music of Marriage

What breath is to the body, communication is to a marriage. Unlike breathing, however, communication is not involuntary, and herein lies the crux of the matter. Not only do we have to choose to communicate, but we must also discipline ourselves to master the skills.

First, we must overcome the language barrier, for as Dr. Deborah Tannen, author of You Just Don't Understand: Women and Men in Conversation, says, "...boys and girls grow up speaking different languages and continue to do so as adults....for girls talk is a way in which intimacy is maintained. A little girl typically has a best friend, and they sit inside and tell each other secrets. And when girls play in groups they tend to make suggestions, rather than give orders, and the suggestions tend to be taken up and tend to be for the good of the group.

"For boys, who are likely to play in larger groups, it is the activity that is central. There are winners and losers, and the groups have a hierarchy. The high-status boys give orders and push the low-status boys around."[1]

As a rule, women tend to be relational, while men tend to be competitive, and the way they communicate reflects these differences. She wants to express her feelings in order to develop an intimate relationship. He wants to tell her why she shouldn't feel the way she feels. Though they both speak English, hers is the language of feelings, while his is the language of power.

Then there's the time factor. As one disillusioned young bride so aptly put it: "Before we married, nothing was more important to him than being together. Now he seems to take me for granted. We never talk anymore. He says that since we live together there is no reason why we should have to make a special effort to spend time together."

Her situation is not unique. Most newlywed couples mistakenly assume that communication will take care of itself. During courtship they talked for hours and hours, why should marriage change that? Maybe it shouldn't, but often it does.

According to author and marriage counselor H. Norman Wright, "...when a couple enters marriage, each person is demanding little but

---

[1]Quoted in an article by Barbara Gamarekian in the Tulsa Tribune, November 11, 1991.

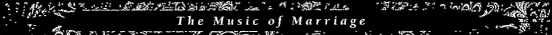

receiving much. Under the influence of very intense feelings, each responds to the other's needs. But in time this changes. More demands are now made on each of them from the outside, whereas previously most of the attention could be focused on their partner. As outside demands increase, we tend to meet less of our spouse's needs in order to fulfill more of our own needs. The couple moves into the stage of giving less and expecting more and unfulfilled needs become a source of conflict."[2]

How a couple handles the resulting conflict will determine, to a significant degree, the quality of their marriage. If they acknowledge what's happening, and take steps to give priority time and energy to their relationship, they can move to a new level of communication. Whereas, during courtship, their communication was based on intensely romantic feelings, it is now based on commitment, an act of their will.

One way to keep the channels of communication open is to have a set time to "check in" with each other.

One couple I know has made a commitment to go to bed together each night. It isn't always easy. Some evenings it means he will miss a late-night sporting event on TV. On other occasions, she will choose to come to bed rather than stay up and watch an old movie.

---

[2]H. Norman Wright, *Seasons of a Marriage* (Ventura: Regal Books, 1982), p. 21.

Although there are times when they would undoubtedly like to do something else, they are both committed to this time together. As he says, "Knowing that we have an appointed time for connecting with each other allows us to pursue our individual responsibilities without fear of drifting apart."

Once in bed, they spend a few minutes "checking in" — catching up on their day, sharing plans for the next day or the coming weekend. She says, "This is not a time for dealing with heavy issues or resolving conflict. Rather, it is a time when we simply open our hearts to one another. After a while we join hands and share a time of prayer. Then we give ourselves to sleep, secure in the knowledge that we are one."

It is not mandatory that your commitment to meaningful communication be exactly like this couple's, or anyone else's for that matter. What is important is that you and your spouse agree together on a regular time and place for the kind of in-depth sharing that renews your marriage. Indeed, it may be the very thing that sustains your marriage in the time of crisis.

For those couples who are truly committed to deep sharing, there remains a level of communication that can only be described as shared privacy.

Because she loves him completely, he can trust her with his life. He tells her his hidden fears, the secret doubts he has never dared share with anyone. In her presence, in the circle of her love, nothing he thinks or says seems insignificant or foolish.

And as he tells her his whole heart — not all at once, but over an extended period — they become one. She takes his life into her own. His joy is now hers. His childhood and adolescence are now part of her past too. His pain is hers as well, and his victories, his achievements, become theirs — the "stuff" of which their oneness is made.

Because he loves her completely, selflessly, she can trust him with her heart. In the quiet of evening, after the children have been put to bed, she tells him the story of her life. Not just the past with its memories, both good and bad, but the events of her day as well. The phone call she received from an old friend, the gist of the conversation she shared with a neighbor over coffee, something one of the children did. Little things, insignificant taken alone, but together they are the fabric of her life. And in the sharing, they become part of his life as well. They become their life — their oneness.

This is the ultimate achievement of marriage — this blessed oneness, the merging of self into self until there can never be one without the other.

Yet in our oneness we lose nothing of our individual personalities. In fact, because of the security of our oneness, each of us is more our

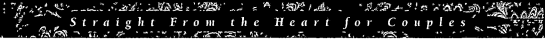

individual self than we have ever been. Freed from the fear of misunderstanding or rejection, we can each truly be the self we were meant to be.

Marital communication is an art, and like other art forms, it requires disciplined practice. Initially, the practice may be tedious and unfulfilling. Many couples drop out or look for shortcuts, but those who stick with it are rewarded with deep and fulfilling relationships. Like a musician who has mastered his instrument, they are free to make beautiful music – and communication is the music of marriage.

4

Celebrating
the Ordinary

*"...the best marriages
are made of moments
like that. Moments when
the simple joy of sharing
life with the one you love
transfuses all of life, even
its painful difficulties,
with a kind of
haunting beauty."*

Chapter 4

Celebrating the Ordinary

In the early days of marriage most of us dream of finishing graduate school and getting established in our careers. We are convinced that life will be better when the pressure is off, when we no longer have to pinch pennies and live in one-bedroom apartments. We are sure that life will be richer and more meaningful when we own a home of our own and can afford a real vacation.

Nothing could be further from the truth. Tough though those early days were they had a vividness, a vitality, that is somehow lacking in the more comfortable present. In the early years we experienced with surprising frequency what, in retrospect, can only be called a sort of epiphany. In the most unexpected places, at the least likely times, life in all of its multi-faceted splendor broke upon us.

Once it happened to Brenda and me while we were eating Church's chicken sitting cross-legged on the floor of the living room with our backs against a roll of carpet. Even now, as I write about it, something of the feeling comes back — a mixture of physical exhaustion and a sense of accomplishment. Night and day, for the better part of three weeks, we had worked to renovate that rundown rental house and finally it was starting to feel like home. Swallowing one last bite of chicken, I leaned back against the roll of carpet and wiped my hands on my soiled jeans. It was a rare moment — a true serendipity, and I felt fulfilled in a deeply satisfying way.

Looking at Brenda I suddenly realized how blessed I was. She had committed herself to me, holding nothing back. Without a complaint, she had followed me from one struggling church to another. She was my closest friend and lover, the mother of my only child. That afternoon, she was wearing jeans and a T-shirt. Her hair was a mess and there was a smudge of paint on her cheek. Still, she had never looked better, and I loved her more than I can say.

From somewhere down the street the sound of children's laughter drifted through our open window. In the distance a dog barked, and belatedly I realized that God was with us. I'm not sure where that thought came from, but suddenly it was there, full-blown and as clear as any thought I've ever had. In a strange sort of way, that unfinished living room became a sanctuary, chicken and corn-on-the-cob, a holy meal, and our conversation a kind of prayer. Even now, more than twenty years later, the memory of that moment has the power to transfix me.

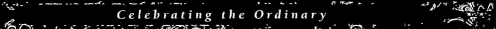

It doesn't happen like that much anymore. Life is too busy, too demanding, too packed with pressure. Still, I long for those sacramental moments when the wonder of life and love transcends the monotony of our days. Such moments can't be forced, I know that, but they can be cultivated.

With determined deliberateness, I do the things that have worked in the past. I brew a cup of coffee. I light the kerosene lamp in my study, I force myself to sit and be quiet. At first, half-a-hundred thoughts wrestle for my attention. Phone calls I need to return. Things I need to do tomorrow, chores that need doing right now.

Resisting the temptation to busyness I wait and out of the stillness comes a picture from the past, indistinct at first, just a dim outline. Then I give myself to it. I embrace it, and it all comes rushing back – the colors, the smells, even the sounds.

It's a Saturday afternoon in early spring and the sky is dark with purple/black thunderheads, foreboding to match my mood. Things aren't going well at the church, but that seems almost inconsequential when I think of the battle Brenda's mother is waging. She has ovarian cancer and is undergoing radiation therapy in a desperate attempt to beat the odds.

Suddenly the setting sun breaks through the dark clouds of the retreating thunderstorm, giving the rain-washed neighborhood a just-

bathed freshness. For a moment, I am transfixed. I forget my half-finished sermon notes, Hildegarde's illness, the problems at the church...everything. I hear Brenda in the kitchen preparing dinner, and suddenly I am at peace.

After a few minutes I write,

"I sit here
in the near darkness
of a late, rain-washed afternoon.
Thunder growls deeply in the distance,
drowning out the sound
of the softly falling rain.

"Yellow light from the kitchen
spills into my mostly dark study,
and I hear you banging pans
and humming softly.

"I feel contented,
but I can remember
when it wasn't so.
When my life was
mostly sadness and shadows,

before the yellow light
of your love came spilling in.

"Now my life is mostly sunshine,
and what sadness remains
huddles in the darkest corners unacknowledged,
unless you are unhappy
or away."

In truth, the best marriages are made of moments like that.
Moments when the simple joy of sharing life with the one you love transfuses all of life, even its painful difficulties, with a kind of haunting beauty. To fully appreciate them, though, you have to take the time. They can
be neither rushed nor postponed.

CHAPTER

5

Love Letters

"*Diamonds may be forever, but nothing touches the heart like a love letter.*"

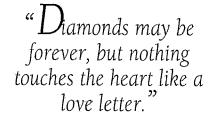

Chapter 5

⌒

Love Letters

*F*lowers are nice, a telephone call is wonderful, but when it comes to expressing the heart's deepest feelings nothing is more effective than a letter. As one husband so aptly put it: "I could have called. It would have been far less trouble, but I would not have put the thought and effort into a call that I put into a letter. Besides, it would have been over in a matter of minutes. The letter she can keep for a lifetime."

And he was right. A telephone call is wonderful, but it does not have the lasting impact of a letter written from the heart. When it's over all you have is a warm feeling and a swiftly fading memory. A letter, on the other hand, can be kept and read again and again, warming the heart each time.

One of the most beautiful letters I've ever seen was written by a devoted husband to his wife on the occasion of their twenty-fifth anniversary. He writes:

"The last twenty-five years have come and gone more quickly than I could have thought possible. The memories we have made are a mixed bag. Some of them are so painful I cannot bear the thought of them. Others are so precious I can hardly speak of them.

How can this be? I sometimes wonder. How can two people create such a hodgepodge of remembrances? It's the nature of life I guess. Still, from this day forward I choose to practice the holy art of selective memory. I choose to forget the painful mistakes of the past while remembering the lessons learned. And having chosen to embrace the joyous memories of our shared past I invite you to journey with me down memory lane.

"I can still remember the first time I saw you, more than thirty years ago. You were only twelve years old, a delicate wisp of a girl, with dark hair and wonderful eyes. You were quiet, but not shy, and by the time you turned fourteen I was wonderfully, crazy, in love with you.

"I remember our first date — my ninth grade football banquet — and the summer we went to Colorado with my mother. We swam in the South Platte River and you got sunburned. I rubbed Noxzema skin cream on your red shoulders and to this day it smells like love to me.

"You were just eighteen when we married, but already a woman in every way. What fun we had, roaming the western half of the United States, preaching in little country churches from Cuero, Texas, to Post Falls, Idaho, and a hundred places in between.

"It seemed we lived in the car. Paul Harvey became a tradition, we discovered Louis L'amour, and you read Charles Spurgeon to me while I drove. Once a snowstorm stranded us in Bozeman, Montana, and you burned your leg on the wall heater trying to get warm after your bath. Still, all in all it was great fun. We were young and so much in love.

"I remember moving into our first home. It was far from new with ancient plumbing, high ceilings and a wheezing floor furnace. We filled it with love and laughter, plus a lot of second-hand furniture. And with God's help we made it a home.

"Do you remember the first time we had guests for dinner? Right after we said grace, you heard a splashing noise in the kitchen, and discovered a mother mouse and her five babies swimming in the soapy dishwater. Without a complaint you did those six mice in. Thankfully, our guests were 'country folk' and unfazed by it all.

"When the moths invaded us each summer, instead of complaining, you turned a miserable situation into a game. After switching off all the lights, you turned on the gas burners, on the kitchen range, and fried those dive-bombing bugs!

"No complaints from you, no tearful depressions, not even envy toward those who were faring better than we. Just an amazing ability to be content in all situations. How fortunate I was. How fortunate I am.

"We celebrated our second anniversary in Colorado and two years later Lori was born and you almost died. We were in Houston for our seventh anniversary and our tenth we celebrated in Steamboat Springs, Colorado. Now we're getting ready to celebrate our twenty-fifth and I can hardly believe it. It seems only yesterday I was watching you come down the center aisle to join me at the altar.

"Lori will be getting married in four months and then it will be just the two of us again. This time I want to show you Maine in the fall and Europe in the spring, and all my love the whole year long.

"You've given me so much — more than I ever imagined possible. Simple things but rare — a quiet place away from the noisy world, a gentle love without demands, inspiration without expectations. Common things too of uncommon value — a cup of coffee when I come home at night, a fire in the fireplace, supper on the stove.

"On this our twenty-fifth anniversary I give you me, now and always. I am yours in a way no one else can ever be yours, in a way I can never be in relationship with anyone else. I will love you all the days of your life. When you are lonely I will comfort you. When you are tired I will refresh you. When you are sick I will care for you. I will share all your days your whole life long. We will celebrate growing old together, warmed against winter's chill by the memories of a lifetime cherished and shared.

With all my love,"

Diamonds may be forever, but nothing touches the heart like a love letter. Who can doubt their value given the fact that virtually every woman has a collection of old love letters stored away in a drawer somewhere or in a trunk in the attic. Not only do they provide a history of their life together, but they afford her the opportunity to relive the joys of their courtship and romance for a lifetime. They remain, as always, love's most enduring expression.

CHAPTER

6

Love and Anger

"*As incongruent as it may be, it seems that in marriage love and anger are joined like Siamese twins.*"

Chapter 6

Love and Anger

Standing at the altar on your wedding day, in the warm glow of your love, you can not imagine hurting your beloved or being hurt by him. The idea that you might sin against her, or she against you, is simply inconceivable.

Unfortunately, the tragic reality of life will soon shatter your romantic idealism. You will sin against your spouse and your marriage, as he or she will sin against you.

More often than not, it will be unintentional. In the press of busyness, one of you will forget a promise made, and the other will feel betrayed. Or one of you will speak sharply, impatiently, like a parent to a dull child, and the other will feel put down. Sometimes one of you will lash out in anger, saying things you don't mean, wounding the very one you love. And, rarely, one of you may sin deliberately, premeditatedly, without regard to the pain you cause.

As incongruent as it may be, it seems that in marriage love and anger are joined like Siamese twins.

According to Howard and Charlotte Clinebell, authors of The Intimate Marriage, "'A relationship which spells closeness also spells conflict.'"[1]

World-renowned marriage and family counselor David R. Mace concurs. He says, "The state of marriage generates in normal people more anger than they are likely to experience in any other type of relationship in which they habitually find themselves."[2]

Although love and anger are poles apart, they are not opposite emotions; rather, they are two sides of the same coin. Love is the positive expression of the deep feelings you have for your spouse, while anger is the negative expression of those very same feelings. It is accurate, I believe, to say that the amount of anger you are capable of feeling is often in direct proportion to how much you love.

Having said that, let me hasten to add that the inappropriate expression of anger is one of the most destructive forces in a relationship.

---

[1] Howard J. Clinebell and Charlotte H. Clinebell, The Intimate Marriage (New York: Harper & Row Publishers, 1970), pp. 95,96.

[2] David Mace, Love and Anger in Marriage (Grand Rapids: Zondervan Publishing House, 1982), p. 12.

Mismanaged, it can tear your marriage apart. No matter how much you love your spouse, it is virtually impossible to overcome the hurt and distrust caused by your reckless anger.

As one emotionally devastated wife so aptly put it: "It takes a hundred kind words to undo the damage from a single angry word."

It is critically important, therefore, that you work to manage the anger in your relationship. Find nondestructive ways of dealing with it. Make it a friend instead of a foe. Learn to make it productive.

Howard and Charlotte Clinebell contend that "a couple can learn to learn from their fights; they can learn how to keep them from becoming physically or emotionally destructive, how to interrupt them sooner and how to grow closer because of them."[3]

They conclude, "Intimacy grows when conflicts are faced and worked through in the painful but fulfilling process of gradual understanding and compromise of differences."[4]

How, you may be wondering, can you make your anger productive instead of destructive?

There is an old story, related by H. Norman Wright, which I believe provides some helpful insight.

---

[3]Howard J. Clinebell and Charlotte H. Clinebell, *The Intimate Marriage* (New York: Harper & Row Publishers, 1970), p. 96.
[4]Ibid.

According to Wright, there was "...a sheepherder in Wyoming who would observe the behavior of wild animals during the winter. Packs of wolves, for example, would sweep into the valley and attack the bands of wild horses. The horses would form a circle with their heads at the center of the circle and kick out at the wolves, driving them away. Then the sheepherder saw the wolves attack a band of wild jackasses. The animals also formed a circle, but they formed it with their heads out toward the wolves. When they began to kick, they ended up kicking one another."[5]

What's the point? You have a choice. You can be as smart as a wild horse, or as stupid as a wild jackass. You can kick the problem, or you can kick each other.

Remember, marital quarrels aren't about winning and losing, but about problem-solving. So stop fighting each other and team up against the problem that is creating the conflict.

One last thought. The most important thing in your marriage is not love, or communication, or understanding or even sexual compatibility. It is forgiveness!

When your spouse has wounded you by some thoughtless word or deed, you must forgive him. If you do not, your hurt will turn into bitterness almost overnight. Forgiving her will not be easy, even if she is

---

[5]H. Norman Wright, *Communication: Key to Your Marriage* (Ventura: Regal Books, 1974), p. 145.

genuinely sorry – but do it anyway. If you cannot do it for your spouse's sake, then do it for yourself and for your marriage.

And perchance if you have sinned against your spouse, take responsibility for your actions. Own your mistake, apologize and seek his or her forgiveness. Apologizing will not undo the damage you have done, but it will give your spouse something to work with. Your apology becomes the raw material out of which he or she fashions the grace to forgive you.

As one frustrated husband said, "I can forgive my wife almost anything if she admits her mistake, but what I can't do is let go of my anger when she refuses to take responsibility for her actions."

When forgiveness is freely given, and fully received, a miracle takes place. Anger dies. Hurt and bitterness are replaced with love. Tenderness takes up residence where hostility once reigned. Communication is restored, and old hurts are replaced by bright hopes. Once again marriage is a safe place in a demanding world.

Keeping Romance
in Marriage

" *Romance is a fragile flower, and it cannot long survive where it is ignored or taken for granted.*"

∽

Chapter 7

∽

Keeping Romance in Marriage

Almost every couple enters marriage with a determination to keep romance alive and well in their relationship. Unfortunately, only a few succeed.

Romance is a fragile flower, and it cannot long survive where it is ignored or taken for granted. Without commitment and imagination, it will slowly wither and die. But for those who are committed to keeping romance in their marriage, the best is yet to come.

It is a wise husband who appreciates his wife's romantic nature and caters to it, though that is not nearly as easy as it sounds. Many of the things that a woman finds romantic are foreign to the average man. Even when he tries to be sensitive and caring, tries to be the romantic husband, he may discover that his best efforts communicate the wrong message.

One young husband, upon the counsel of an older and supposedly wiser man, bought his wife an expensive night-gown four years running. Much to his chagrin she became tearfully angry upon receiving her fourth night-gown in as many years. Refusing it, she said, "All you ever buy me are negligees. And it's not even for me, not really."

"What do you mean it's not for you?" he demanded, more confused than angry.

"It's for you," she said. "I'm supposed to put it on and look sexy — for you, for your pleasure. Then we'll make love, and I'll feel used. Just once I wish you would buy me a new dress."

The issue wasn't a new dress, though that would have been nice. What his wife wanted, and needed, was a public demonstration of his love — something that said to the world, "I love this woman. I'm glad she's my wife."

Now, a new dress is not the only way to do that, and not necessarily the best way. Many a husband has discovered that small gestures of affection, like holding his wife's hand in public, or taking her arm as they cross the street, make her feel special, as does a timely compliment. And you can be assured that feeling special is an important part of romance, especially to a woman.

It is a wise wife who understands that her husband is not naturally romantic. When he brought her flowers and wrote her poetry during their courtship, he was acting out of character in order to win her love. He does not love her less now that they are married, but neither does he see the

importance of continuing his romantic gestures. As far as he is concerned, they were for another time and place.

Though she may well feel slighted, she must not take his lack of romance personally. It is not directed toward her, but is simply a reflection of who he is. If she nags him, he will probably retreat into a stubborn shell. However, if she is patient and imaginative, she can encourage him to become romantic.

Let her make their time together special. Even if dinner is a simple meal, she can serve it by candlelight with mood music. She can invite him to go for a walk or to watch a sunset. Of course, it would be nice if he initiated these romantic gestures, but if he doesn't she should. In time he may even learn to take the lead.

Many couples have found it important to schedule a weekly night out. It is their time together. They may go to dinner, see a movie, take in a concert or attend a sporting event. What they do is not as important as the fact that they are together, just the two of them. Occasionally, they may "double date," but even then they make a special effort to pay attention to each other. She holds his hand under the table, he puts his arm around her in the movie; this is their night and nothing must distract from it.

Other couples have found less traditional ways of keeping romance in their marriage. One caring husband turns down the bed each night

and warms his wife's side of the bed so she doesn't have to crawl between cold sheets. A creative wife keeps a journal of special events and reads it each year on their anniversary, providing not only a priceless history of their life together, but also the nostalgic joy of memories relived. Another couple returns to their honeymoon suite each anniversary.

Do the unexpected.

One wife says she will never forget the day her husband came in with a half a dozen red roses and said, "Pack your bag. We're leaving in thirty minutes."

Off they went to a quaint little hotel in the Vienna woods about thirty minutes from where they lived. Her husband had previously chosen the hotel and told them he had a very special lady friend he wanted to bring for a weekend getaway. To this day she is convinced the hotel staff didn't think they were married. Her husband's response? "If you're going to have a romantic affair, have it with your mate!"[1]

In marriage, little things mean a lot, especially to a woman. In fact, they can make the difference between a mediocre marriage and a really good one, one in which romance is alive and well.

---

[1]Dave and Claudia Arp, "Learning to Say the 'S' Word or Building a Creative Love Life," taken from The Marriage Track and quoted in The Making of a Marriage (Nashville: Thomas Nelson Publishers, 1993), p. 178.

It's usually not the expensive gifts or the foreign vacations that determine the quality of a marital relationship, but the little things. A love note or an "unbirthday" card. A kind word, help with the children, a listening ear, the feeling that you really care. This is the stuff of which marital romance is made!

C H A P T E R

8

Love for a Lifetime

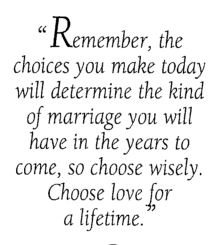

"*Remember, the choices you make today will determine the kind of marriage you will have in the years to come, so choose wisely. Choose love for a lifetime.*"

Chapter 8

Love for a Lifetime

Some time ago my father underwent his second bypass surgery. It was an enormously stressful time for all of us, yet in the midst of that crisis I witnessed love as pure and selfless as I ever hope to see. No single act stands out in my mind above the others; rather, it is a mosaic.

I see my mother bending over my father's bed in the intensive care unit reserved for cardiac surgery patients. He is hardly recognizable, resembling not at all the man we kissed good-bye just hours ago. Now his motionless body is fairly entangled with medical devices: a breathing tube, a catheter, a drainage tube, an IV. In addition, he is connected by a complexity of leads to a heart monitor which records his cardiac functions with squiggly lines on a green monitor.

All in all, it is more than a little disconcerting.

Mother seems not to notice as she bends over him, whispering her love in words he cannot hear. Locating an unencumbered area on his arm, she strokes his skin tenderly. With her other hand she smooths his hair down. Standing beside her, I think, so this is what love looks like after nearly half a century.

Far too soon, a nurse comes and ushers us out, telling us that we can see him again, for fifteen minutes, in three hours.

Out in the hall, once more Mother blinks back tears and pretends to be brave. "He looks good, real good," she says, trying to assuage her fears as much as to reassure the rest of us. As she talks, I see her the way she was this morning when they came to take Dad down to surgery.

The nurse is the consummate professional. Without wasting a motion, she gets Dad transferred from the bed onto the gurney. As he is rolled into the corridor, she tells Mother that she should go ahead and tell Dad good-bye as there is no reason for us to ride down with him. Mother thanks her, but doesn't even consider her suggestion.

To the nurse, Dad is just another in a long line of patients scheduled for heart surgery this April day. To Mother, he is a beloved husband, the father of her children and her very best friend. No matter what the nurse says, she is not about to leave him until he enters the operating room itself.

Once that's settled, we all crowd into the elevator, much to the dismay of the nurse who sees our devotion as an unnecessary complication in her already demanding day. Although she says nothing, her disapproval

is obvious. Ignoring her, Mother holds Dad's hand and gazes into his eyes as the elevator makes its slow descent.

Just outside the double doors leading to the operating room, Mother bends to kiss Dad one final time. For the briefest moment I think she is going to lose her composure, but then she quickly regains it. The look she gives Dad as he is rolled away is filled with such compassion that I cannot help thinking that if love could heal, my father would rise from that gurney a whole man.

It is now almost 7:00 P.M., and we have been at the hospital nearly fourteen hours. Although it is a forty-five-minute drive to the folks' house, we decide to go home and rest for a few minutes before returning to the hospital at nine for our allotted quarter-hour visit.

Thus begins a three-day odyssey in which we return to the hospital every three hours so Mother can be with Dad for fifteen minutes. During one of our brief visits, a nurse tells me that she has never seen a more devoted wife. As she walks away, I cannot help thinking of the wedding vows, "...in sickness and in health, to love and to cherish, till death us do part..." Seldom have they seemed so real.

On the third day as we are about to leave for the hospital, we receive a call informing us that my father has been moved into a private room. Mother is like a schoolgirl in her excitement as she packs a suitcase and prepares to join Dad at the hospital for the duration of his stay. The suitcase she chooses is fairly large, and when I pick it up to take it to the car, I stagger at its weight.

"What do you have in here?" I demand in mock anger.

It turns out that she has packed seven complete outfits for herself, as well as several pairs of pajamas for Dad, and her own nightwear. In addition, she has packed both of their Bibles, a devotional book, The Pentecostal Evangel, Guideposts and various other reading materials. When I question why she needs so many outfits, she informs me that she is not leaving the hospital until Dad is released. Nor does she do so until she leaves with him six days later.

I stay one more day, and then I have to catch a flight to take care of my own commitments. Telling Mom and Dad good-bye, I suddenly find myself weeping. For a minute I do not know why. Dad's prognosis is good, and he is in no immediate danger. Then it hits me. These tears are not for them. They are for me. I am crying because something deep inside me yearns to be loved the way my mother loves my father.

I hear myself praying, "Oh, God, help Brenda to love me like that." Ever so gently, but ever so clearly, the Holy Spirit convicts me, and now I pray, "Oh, God, help me to love Brenda like that."

Now, I believe with all my heart that this is what God had in mind when He said, "...'It is not good for the man to be alone. I will make a helper suitable for him.'"[1]

Yet a marriage like that doesn't just happen. It is built over the course of a lifetime, one act, one decision at a time.

What we do today, good or bad, will become the material out of which we build our future. Unkind words, thoughtless deeds, broken promises, a trust betrayed, will become cornerstones in a marriage haunted by old hurts and present fears. Gentle words, acts of kindness, a promise kept, a love that is true, these will become the cornerstones in a marriage built by love.

Remember, the choices you make today will determine the kind of marriage you will have in the years to come, so choose wisely. Choose love for a lifetime.

---

[1]Genesis 2:18.

Epilogue

On November 5, 1994, our daughter Leah Starr was married in a beautiful ceremony on Emerald Point (our hideaway in the Ozarks).

On the day of Leah's wedding, her Grandmother Wallace wrote her a touching letter filled with the wisdom of her sixty-eight years. Although she received only the most limited formal education, she possesses remarkable insight and a rare wisdom. With her permission, I share her letter and the wisdom she gleaned during fifty years of marriage.

Our Dearest Leah Starr and Douglas:

Leah, from the first day Grandpa and I saw you in the hospital nursery in Syracuse, Kansas, a love was born that words cannot describe. We look into a flower, a beautiful sunset, read a lovely poem, still there are no words to describe what we feel for you.

It was wonderful to be your first nurse. You and I got along great — you learned when to sleep real quick because I held you close and loved you so much. I hope we have always been the kind of grandparents you needed, and I pray we never fail you.

You may be all grown up now, but you are still my grandbaby, and you always will be, even after you are married. Today is your wedding day so let me pass along some of the things Grandpa and I have learned.

Some may say old people don't know much about love, but we do — fifty years of love. We have tasted much — roses, thorns, sunshine and rain — but I love Grandpa more today than the day I married him (when his hair was as black as Douglas' hair is now).

When we first married, we left God out, and it wasn't working. Once we turned to Him, everything changed for the better. I know that sometimes that doesn't work, but it is because both persons haven't made a true commitment to the Lord. If you and Douglas always put God first in your marriage, you can overcome anything.

Getting married is wonderful and also scary. A marriage may be made in heaven, but the maintenance must be done on earth. May you always consider each other first, before others.

Don't destroy each other with words, especially in public. Words are very powerful, they can kill love faster than roses can mend it. Always work toward the best for each other. Never leave each other without a kiss or an "I love you." Three little words, but they mean so much. Respect each other or the stars won't come out at night. Even in a crowd always let each other know you are aware of them.

We love you both very much and ask God's best for you. We know you love each other and God — a never-failing formula.

You and Douglas have a lifetime ahead of you, should Jesus tarry. Grandpa and I are old, and someday you will be called to a funeral and then we will be waiting for you in heaven. That's why we always tell you about the best way — because we want the best for you here and in the life to come, which is more real than this one.

Leah, I could never end this letter, but I must stop now and get ready for your wedding. I guess I should have started sooner. Oh, well...

Remember, loving real close brings a lot of good things. Loving real close will bring happiness to you and Douglas. Loving Jesus real close will take you to heaven.

> Your loving Grandpa
> and Grandma Wallace

Other books by Richard Exley
are available at your local bookstore.

Straight From the Heart for Mom

Straight From the Heart for Dad

Straight From the Heart for Graduates

How to Be a Man of Character
in a World of Compromise

Marriage in the Making

The Making of a Man

Abortion

Blue-Collar Christianity

Life's Bottom Line

Perils of Power

The Rhythm of Life

When You Lose Someone You Love

The Other God —
Seeing God as He Really Is

The Painted Parable

Tulsa, Oklahoma

To contact the author, write:

Richard Exley
P.O. Box 54744
Tulsa, Oklahoma 74155

Please include your prayer requests
when you write.

Tulsa, Oklahoma